W9-BBK-469

THE CASELOAD OF THE SUPREME COURT
And What, If Anything, To Do About It

Alexander M. Bickel

American Enterprise Institute for Public Policy Research
Washington, D. C.

Alexander M. Bickel is Chancellor Kent professor of law and legal history, Yale Law School.

347.9973

B47c

8 6826

Jan. 1974

ISBN 0-8447-3121-8

Domestic Affairs Study 21, November 1973

Library of Congress Catalog Card No. L.C. 73-91329

Printed in the United States of America

CONTENTS

THE CASELOAD OF
THE SUPREME COURT

1. A Sketch of the Historical Background

Article III, the judiciary article of the Constitution, vests the judicial power of the United States "in one supreme Court" and in "inferior" (lower) federal courts. But it was left to Congress to organize the Supreme Court, to establish the lower courts, and to distribute the federal judicial power among them. Congress acted promptly. The Judiciary Act of 1789 provided for a chief justice of the United States and five associate justices of the Supreme Court, and it established lower federal courts, one set of them consisting of a district judge and two Supreme Court justices each. The justices were required, as the phrase went, to "ride circuit."

Broadly speaking, the jurisdiction granted to these lower federal courts covered civil litigation between citizens of different states (though not all such litigation of which jurisdiction could have been granted under the Constitution), certain cases in which aliens were parties, "all civil causes of admiralty and maritime jurisdiction," cases in which the United States was the plaintiff, and federal criminal cases. But the first Judiciary Act did not give the lower federal courts what is today an enormously important jurisdiction, qualitatively and quantitatively, namely, jurisdiction to hear civil cases in which claims of right are made under the Constitution or laws of the United States. Even though the Constitution authorized the Congress to confer this jurisdiction, then as now, Congress did not confer it full-blown on the lower federal courts until 1875.

The appellate jurisdiction of the Supreme Court, as prescribed by the Judiciary Act of 1789, covered most but not all of the business confided to the lower federal courts. Thus the Supreme Court was not given jurisdiction to review any criminal cases arising in the lower federal courts, and it was granted jurisdiction in civil cases only if "the matter in dispute exceeds the sum or value of two thousand dollars, exclusive of costs." But the Supreme Court was given jurisdiction to review cases coming from the highest courts of the states where a federal statute, treaty or other exercise of federal authority had been declared invalid; or where a state statute or other exercise of state authority had been challenged under the federal Constitution, treaties or laws and held valid; or where any claim of right made under the federal Constitution, or a treaty, statute or other exercise of federal authority had been denied.

The system established by the Judiciary Act of 1789 grew as the country grew. It underwent some changes dictated by its own logic, and it was occasionally just tinkered with. But its essential structure remained intact for 100 years. The obligation to ride circuit, a most onerous burden in the conditions of the time, was somewhat relaxed in 1802. In 1802 also, Congress provided an interesting additional method of review of decisions of the lower federal courts by the Supreme Court, which endured until 1872 and which still endures in modified fashion, although it is rarely used. As noted above, the act of 1789 had given the Supreme Court automatic appellate jurisdiction only if the value of the matter in controversy exceeded $2,000. In 1802 it was provided that if there was a division of opinion in a lower court, the judges could in their discretion certify the question that divided them to the Supreme Court for decision, regardless of the monetary value of the matter in dispute. In criminal cases, moreover, in which there was no automatic appellate jurisdiction at all, judges of the lower courts were required to certify an issue on which they were divided to the Supreme Court for decision. But it remained true until 1891 that criminal cases were not ordinarily reviewable in the Supreme Court.

In 1807, the number of associate justices of the Supreme Court was raised to six, making a total of seven members of the Court including the chief justice. In 1837, the total was raised to nine, where it has remained except for some juggling of numbers up and down during the Civil War years. All through the nineteenth century, the volume of business increased steadily. New sources of jurisdiction were added, and the Court's appellate jurisdiction was expanded, although always with some exceptions for those classes of cases in which no access was provided.

By 1870, the system was thoroughly clogged. "Legislation concerning judicial organization throughout our history," Felix Frankfurter and James M. Landis found upon looking back in 1928, "has been a very empiric response to very definite needs."[1] On more than one occasion, however, definite needs became pressing and the "empiric response" lagged. This was the situation during the two decades before passage of the Court of Appeals Act of 1891. Between 1870 and 1880, the number of cases in the Supreme Court of the United States nearly doubled—from 636 to 1,212. By the beginning of the Court's October term, 1890, the number had risen to 1,816. This increase reflected, of course, a like explosion in the lower federal courts.

The empiric response came at last. The Court of Appeals Act of 1891 divided the country into nine circuits (there are now eleven, including the District of Columbia circuit) and established in each an intermediate federal court of appeals consisting initially of three judges (in all but one circuit there are now many more). In a substantial category of cases, the decisions of the circuit courts of appeals were to be "final." Further review in the Supreme Court of the United States could be had only in that Court's discretion, by the grant of a writ of certiorari.[2] Automatic appeals could still be taken, however, in other classes of federal cases and from state courts. Yet the volume of such appeals was considerably reduced. "The remedy was decisive. The Supreme Court at once felt its benefits. . . . While in the October Term, 1887, 482 new cases were docketed . . . and in 1890, 623; in 1891 (with the new act only a few months in operation) new business dropped to 379 cases, and in 1892 to 275 cases."[3]

The remedy was decisive, but not for long. It came just as the country was about to enter a period of extensive federal legislative activity, which naturally produced judicial business. The number of appeals in cases from state and federal courts in which review by the Supreme Court remained automatic, that is, as of right, or had newly been made so, kept increasing, even though the discretionary segment of the Court's jurisdiction was enlarged by the Judiciary Act of 1916.

---

[1] F. Frankfurter and J. M. Landis, *The Business of the Supreme Court* (New York: Johnson Reprint Corp., 1928), p. 13.

[2] A writ of certiorari is an order from a superior court calling up the record of a proceeding in a lower court for review. In current practice before the United States Supreme Court, a petition for a writ of certiorari is the most frequent means of requesting the Supreme Court to review a lower court's decision. Review under this procedure is granted at the discretion of the Supreme Court. The Court's practice is to grant a writ of certiorari if at least four justices vote in favor of its issuance.

[3] Frankfurter and Landis, *Business of the Supreme Court*, pp. 101-102.

The volume of petitions for certiorari also rose steadily—from 270 at the October term, 1916, to 456 at the 1924 term. Under the leadership of Chief Justice William Howard Taft, therefore, some thirty years after the act of 1891, a committee of the Court drafted and the Congress eventually passed what was known as the Judges' Bill of 1925. This statute, which is still in effect, converted most—though even yet not all—of the Court's jurisdiction to a discretionary rather than an obligatory one, to be invoked by the filing of a petition for a writ of certiorari. A small and continually decreasing percentage of these petitions is granted, and the Court then hears and decides the cases involved. In the vast majority of cases, the Court denies the petition. Cases remaining in the Court's obligatory jurisdiction also arrive initially in the form of what amounts to a petition for review, and the Court makes a preliminary decision whether the appeal is a proper one.

A significant portion of the Court's present obligatory jurisdiction was first introduced in 1903, and it continued to be obligatory rather than discretionary even after enactment of the Judges' Bill of 1925. In 1903 Congress created special three-judge trial courts for antitrust and some other federal regulatory cases, from which a direct and obligatory appeal lay to the Supreme Court itself. A few years later, three-judge courts were required also to hear cases in which the enforcement of a state statute was sought to be enjoined, and again there was an obligatory appeal to the Supreme Court of the United States. The idea has prospered. The realm of three-judge courts has increased, new categories of cases being added over the years, and the volume of three-judge court litigation with direct obligatory appeal to the Supreme Court has swelled.

Nonetheless, the remedy of the Judges' Bill of 1925 was also decisive in its time; but also only for a time.[4]

2. The Present Problem

It need come as no surprise to anyone that the business of the Supreme Court, and of the lower federal courts and the state courts as well, has continued to burgeon. Moreover, in the past two decades for the Supreme Court and in the past five years for the lower federal

---

[4] A concise summary of the historical developments touched on in this section will be found in P. M. Bator, E. J. Mishkin, D. L. Shapiro, and H. Wechsler, in H. M. Hart and Wechsler, eds., *The Federal Courts and the Federal System* (Mineola, N. Y.: The Foundation Press, 1973), pp. 32-46. The standard text on the subject is Frankfurter and Landis, *Business of the Supreme Court*.

courts, the growth has been explosive. The reasons for this are obvious. The country has grown. All that we do is more complex and more intricately interrelated. We touch and jostle each other more than we used to when there were fewer of us and our activities were simpler. We need more regulation—and have it whether we need it or not. Laws have multiplied, and law has expanded.

The number of cases on the Supreme Court's docket approximately tripled from the 1951 term to the 1971 term, and the rate of increase was much greater in the second of these two decades. At the 1951 term, the Court had 1,353 cases before it clamoring for review. At the 1961 term, the number was 2,570. At the 1971 term, it was 4,515. A year later at the 1972 term, which ended in June 1973, the number had increased to 4,619. Another equally telling way to gauge the volume is to look at the figures for new cases— appeals and petitions for certiorari—filed each year. (The figures just given include a carry-over from year to year.) In 1951, the number of new cases filed was 1,234. At the 1961 term it had risen to 2,185, at the 1971 term to 3,643, and at the 1972 term to 3,741.

The trend indicated by these figures is clearly continuing. The best evidence of this is the shape of the iceberg of which the docket of the Supreme Court is the tip. In the four years from 1968 to 1972, total filings of cases in federal district courts increased from 102,163 to 143,216, which comes to roughly an increase of 10,000 cases a year. In the same period, filings in the federal courts of appeals, which had more than doubled from 1961 to 1968, increased by over 5,000—from 9,116 to 14,535. This four-year increase alone was substantially greater than the total number of cases filed in the courts of appeals in 1961.

The consequences for the Supreme Court are summarized by Judge Henry J. Friendly of the Court of Appeals for the Second Circuit: "If I am right in thinking that, unless the intake in the district courts is restricted, the filings in the courts of appeals will pass the 20,000 mark well before the end of the decade, the Supreme Court will then have some 3,400 petitions for certiorari from these courts alone—as many as the Court's entire filings for the 1969 Term."[5] Assuming that present ratios are maintained, these 3,400 petitions from the circuit courts would constitute something under 70 percent of the Supreme Court's docket, as some 30 percent of the Court's cases come from the state courts. If the intake in the district

[5] H. J. Friendly, *Federal Jurisdiction: A General View* (New York and London: Columbia University Press, 1973), pp. 48-49; for the statistics of cases filed in the lower federal courts, see ibid., pp. 16-17 and 31-32.

courts should somehow be restricted, the problem of the size of the Supreme Court's docket would perhaps be somewhat alleviated, but not substantially, since in great measure the effect would be merely to change the avenues by which cases reach the Supreme Court, not to prevent them reaching it.

These figures speak for themselves, but what do they tell us? Similar or even more forbidding figures could be adduced to show exponential growth in the business of executive and legislative agencies of government. Yet we manage generally to suppress a sense of crisis and do not seek ways of protecting an overburdened agency from the flood of business. Rather we cope. The agency acquires additional mechanical aids, where appropriate, and additional staff, and it carries on. The questions that the figures on judicial business raise are whether courts are different—and most particularly whether the Supreme Court of the United States is different—from, say, the Department of Health, Education, and Welfare, the Civil Aeronautics Board, or the Federal Power Commission, and whether, therefore, a sense of crisis or at least impending crisis is appropriate and remedies of a fundamental nature are required.

3. The Study Group on the Caseload of the Supreme Court and Its Proposed Solutions

In telling the story of the Judges' Bill of 1925, the reform for which Chief Justice Taft deserved so much credit, Felix Frankfurter and James M. Landis remarked that "unlike some of his predecessors," Taft "deemed it the prerogative and even the duty of his office to take the lead in promoting judicial reform and to wait neither upon legislative initiation in Congress nor upon professional opinion."[6] Taft's successor, Chief Justice Charles Evans Hughes, presided over the beneficial effects of the reforms of the Taft era. Chief Justices Harlan F. Stone and Fred M. Vinson, who followed Hughes, each served relatively briefly and at a time when the Taft reforms still worked well. It was in the latter part of the tenure of Chief Justice Earl Warren, who succeeded Vinson, that problems again began to emerge. They were there, unmistakable and getting worse, when Chief Justice Warren E. Burger took office in 1969. Like Taft, and unlike his intermediate predecessors who confronted no exigency of equal proportion, Chief Justice Burger deems it the duty of his office to take the lead in promoting judicial reform.

---

[6] Frankfurter and Landis, *Business of the Supreme Court*, pp. 259-260.

In the fall of 1972 Chief Justice Burger established a Study Group on the Caseload of the Supreme Court. The chief justice appointed the study group in his capacity as chairman of the Federal Judicial Center, an institution created by Congress in 1968 and charged among other things with the function of conducting "research and study of the operation of the courts of the United States." In choosing the members of the study group, Chief Justice Burger has since remarked, "the conclusion was reached that it should be a relatively small group but one that would embrace a wide range of Supreme Court experience." He added that the seven lawyers appointed, four of them teachers of law, were all "practitioners before the Supreme Court, their period of practice going back forty years. Three members of the committee were selected in part because they had been clerks to Justices of the Supreme Court"—one forty, another twenty, and the third a dozen years ago.[7]

The group's chairman was Professor Paul A. Freund of Harvard Law School. Its members were Peter D. Ehrenhaft of the District of Columbia bar; Russell D. Niles, former dean of the New York University Law School and now director of the Institute of Judicial Administration in New York; Bernard G. Segal of the Philadelphia bar, former president of the American Bar Association; Robert L. Stern of the Chicago bar, former acting solicitor general of the United States; Professor Charles Alan Wright of the University of Texas Law School; and the present writer.

The study group pursued its task for a full year. It met with each of the justices of the Supreme Court and, in addition, interviewed three law clerks whose experience was fresh: one who was then in the service of the chief justice and two who had just completed service, respectively, with the late Justice Black and the late Justice Harlan. The group collected data from the Office of the Clerk of the Supreme Court and drew on the resources of the Federal Judicial Center. In December 1972, the study group issued a report.

The report begins by addressing the question that is left open, as noted above, by the statistics concerning the Court's business, namely, are the consequences of the rise in the volume of business, and therefore the indicated response, different in the case of the Supreme Court than in the case, for example, of the Department of Health, Education, and Welfare or the Federal Power Commission? An answer to this question depends fundamentally on one's premise

---

[7] "Retired Chief Justice Warren Attacks, Chief Justice Burger Defends Freund Study Group's Composition and Proposal," *American Bar Association Journal*, vol. 59 (July 1973), p. 721.

about the nature of the Court's function, which is why the study group led off by stating its own premise. This statement deserves quite full quotation, since from it much else flows.

Any assessment of the Court's workload will be affected by the conception that is held of the Court's function in our judicial system and in our national life. We accept and underscore the traditional view that the Supreme Court is not simply another court of errors and appeals. Its role is a distinctive and essential one in our legal and constitutional order: to define and vindicate the rights guaranteed by the Constitution, to assure the uniformity of federal law, and to maintain the constitutional distribution of powers in our federal union.

The cases which it is the primary duty of the Court to decide are those that, by hypothesis, present the most fundamental and difficult issues of law and judgment. To secure the uniform application of federal law the Court must resolve problems on which able judges in lower courts have differed among themselves. To maintain the constitutional order the Court must decide controversies that have sharply divided legislators, lawyers, and the public. And in deciding, the Court must strive to understand and elucidate the complexities of the issues, to give direction to the law, and to be as precise, persuasive, and invulnerable as possible in its exposition. The task of decision must clearly be a process, not an event, a process at the opposite pole from the "processing" of cases in a high-speed, high-volume enterprise. The indispensable condition for the discharge of the Court's responsibility is adequate time and ease of mind for research, reflection, and consultation in reaching a judgment, for critical review by colleagues when a draft opinion is prepared, and for clarification and revision in light of all that has gone before.[8]

The report proceeds to assess the volume and nature of the Court's business and notes the line of its growth and the measures taken in the past, such as the Court of Appeals Act of 1891 and the Judges' Bill of 1925, to relieve the pressure. These previous solutions, the report finds, have now become "part of the problem." The conclusion drawn in the report is as follows:

The statistics of the Court's current workload, both in absolute terms and in the mounting trend, are impressive evidence that the conditions essential for the performance

---

[8] *Report of the Study Group on the Caseload of the Supreme Court* (Washington, D. C.: Federal Judicial Center, 1972), p. 1; hereinafter *Report.*

of the Court's mission do not exist. For an ordinary appellate court the burgeoning volume of cases would be a staggering burden; for the Supreme Court the pressures of the docket are incompatible with the appropriate fulfillment of its historic and essential functions.[9]

Remedies Rejected by the Study Group. The report then surveys some of the possible remedies that the study group rejected, and outlines the reasons why they were rejected:

Additional law clerks. Three clerks are now authorized for each justice. Adding more would be no solution so long as the responsibilities of each justice continued to be nondelegable. The drawback of adding law clerks would be to accelerate a tendency in each expanding office to "turn the center of gravity inward . . . depersonalize the work, and jeopardize the collegial character of the Court's labors," with the end result of changing the Court into a "federation of nine corporate aggregates or chambers."[10]

Division of the Court into panels. It is questionable whether this scheme is permissible under Article III of the Constitution, which establishes "one supreme Court." Moreover, chance would necessarily govern the composition of each panel sitting for any case or group of cases, and an element of a lottery would thus be introduced which would weaken the authority of the Court.

A constitutional court. Limiting the jurisdiction of the Supreme Court to cases presenting constitutional issues would deprive the country of the final judgment of the Supreme Court on many issues of prime importance which are not constitutional—and there are such issues—and would sacrifice flexibility and resourcefulness in determining the grounds of decision in that very large number of cases in which constitutional and nonconstitutional issues are intertwined.

Exclusion of classes of cases. It is very difficult to say that any class of litigation now within the Supreme Court's jurisdiction could never bring to the Court a case important enough for review by it. Hence the absolute foreclosure of review in any category of cases would be unwise.

Specialized courts of administrative appeals. This could be a worthwhile reform of great help in alleviating the burdens now resting on lower federal courts, although it is not without its drawbacks. But it would have little if any impact on the volume of business

---

[9] Ibid., pp. 8, 5.
[10] Ibid., p. 7.

confronting the Supreme Court. It would merely change the origin of some of the business.

A court of criminal appeals.[11] Like any other specialized court, a court of criminal appeals would relieve the Supreme Court of a substantial burden of business only if its decisions were made final, with no possibility of review by the Supreme Court. To whatever extent this were done, the result would be that defendants in criminal cases would be placed in an unacceptable "inferior and invidious position with respect to access to the Supreme Court."[12]

Certification for review by lower courts. Conditioning Supreme Court review upon such certification would be a method of screening likely to "lack coherence, and [which] might at times lack as well, and more often appear to lack, objectivity."[13]

A senior screening staff.[14] A senior staff, which would be appointed by the Court and would be charged with initial examination of all cases filed and with making recommendations to the Court whether to accept cases for review or not, would fail to relieve the pressure on the justices so long as they retained the responsibility for decision. Having that responsibility, the justices would feel obliged to exercise it, as they do now, when recommendations come to them from their own law clerks. On the other hand, if the justices should be not merely assisted, as they are now by law clerks, but substantially relieved of the burden of decision, because in practice the justices would generally accept the recommendations of a senior screening staff as a matter of course, then public confidence in the Court would be impaired.[15]

---

[11] See C. F. Haynsworth, Jr., "A New Court to Improve the Administration of Justice," *American Bar Association Journal*, vol. 59 (August 1973), p. 841.

[12] *Report*, p. 12.

[13] Ibid., p. 15.

[14] See N. O. Stockmeyer, Jr., "Rx for the Certiorari Crisis: A More Professional Staff," *American Bar Association Journal*, vol. 59 (August 1973), p. 846.

[15] Since the study group's report was issued, it has become known that some justices have pooled their law clerks on an experimental basis and have been receiving, as a group, memoranda from the pool. Cases are assigned to law clerks in the pool on a rotating basis. Other members of the Court have declined to enter into this arrangement, believing that they can be assisted only by clerks under their own supervision. See P. A. Freund, "Why We Need the National Court of Appeals," *American Bar Association Journal*, vol. 59 (March 1973), pp. 247-250.

The Court's budget request to Congress for fiscal 1974 includes a request for the creation of three positions of senior career legal assistant, one each for three justices who are not named.

A fourth-tier appellate court. One proposal calls for a court intermediate between the present courts of appeals and the Supreme Court which would hear, and render final decision in, cases referred to it by the Supreme Court as well as a category of cases coming to it initially. This proposal—for an additional half-tier, really, not a fourth—would not substantially relieve the Supreme Court of the burden of its docket. But a full-fledged fourth tier would do so, and most effectively. It would involve creation of a new national court of review composed of fifteen judges and sitting in three sections, civil, administrative, and criminal. Such a court would have the full jurisdiction that the Supreme Court now has and equal discretion in choosing cases for decision. The sole appellate jurisdiction of the Supreme Court would be to review the decisions of this new court. The docket of the Supreme Court would therefore be restricted to the perhaps 450 or so cases that the new court would decide each year. This change, adding another stage of litigation for some hundreds of cases each year, was considered too drastic by the study group and still avoidable, although quite possibly its time might eventually come.

Recommendations of the Study Group. Such were the principal ideas that the study group rejected. Its own recommendations were four in number, of which the last three are best given in the words of the study group's summary:

> 2. The elimination by statute of three-judge district courts and direct review of their decisions in the Supreme Court; the elimination also of direct appeals in ICC [Interstate Commerce Commission] and antitrust cases; and the substitution of certiorari for appeal in all cases where appeal is now the prescribed procedure for review in the Supreme Court. . . .
>
> 3. The establishment by statute of a non-judicial body whose members would investigate and report on complaints of prisoners, both collateral attacks on convictions and complaints of mistreatment in prison. Recourse to this procedure would be available to prisoners before filing a petition in a federal court, and to the federal judges with whom petitions were filed.
>
> 4. Increased staff support for the Supreme Court in the Clerk's office and the Library, and improved secretarial facilities for the Justices and their law clerks.[16]

---

[16] _Report,_ pp. 47-48.

The first and chief recommendation is more complex. It is that a new National Court of Appeals be established to screen all cases in which ultimate Supreme Court review is sought and to itself decide one category of cases. The composition of such a court, the study group suggested, could be determined in a number of ways. The group's own recommendation was that the new court be composed of seven judges, drawn on a rotating basis from the existing federal courts of appeals and serving staggered three-year terms. The National Court would sit in Washington, although its members could continue to maintain residence in their circuits if they chose. Its jurisdiction would be coextensive with the present jurisdiction of the Supreme Court, except for the Court's original jurisdiction (which involves just a few cases each year, mainly suits against or between states).

Thus all cases that are now within the Supreme Court's jurisdiction, except for that small group of original cases, would be filed initially in the new National Court, exactly as they are now filed in the Supreme Court directly. The National Court would have discretion to deny review on the basis of the criteria now used by the Supreme Court itself and mentioned in the Rules of the Supreme Court, or on the basis of such other criteria as the Supreme Court might lay down in further rules for the guidance of the National Court. Denial of review in the National Court would be final, and there would be no access to the Supreme Court. The National Court would also have discretion, again guided by the criteria the Supreme Court now employs or by further criteria the Supreme Court might lay down, to certify a case to the Supreme Court for disposition.

In cases in which a circuit court of appeals rendered a decision in conflict with a decision of another circuit court of appeals, the National Court would certify the case to the Supreme Court if in its judgment the conflict of decisions between circuit courts was real and if the issues in the case were of sufficient importance. If in the judgment of the National Court the conflict was real but the issues were not important enough in light of the criteria governing Supreme Court review, then the National Court would set the case down for argument and proceed to decide it itself. Its decision would be final.

The expectation would be that all cases that raised any serious doubt would be certified to the Supreme Court, and that, therefore, several times more cases than the Supreme Court could be expected to hear and decide each year would be certified—somewhere perhaps between 400 and 500 cases annually, the study group estimated. These cases would constitute the appellate docket of the Supreme

Court, except that the Court would retain the power that it now has (but rarely exercises) to bring a case up for review before judgment in a court of appeals and before denial of review in the National Court.

Once a case had arrived in the Supreme Court it would be disposed of there by a grant of review or a denial of review, by a grant of limited review, or by reversal or affirmance without argument. Additionally, in a case involving a conflict of decisions between different circuit courts of appeals, the Supreme Court, if it agreed that the conflict was a real one but did not view the issues presented as being of sufficient comparative importance to warrant decision in the Supreme Court itself, could grant review and remand the case to the National Court with an order that that court hear and adjudicate it.

"We are aware of objections that can be raised against this recommendation," said the Study Group on the Caseload of the Supreme Court. "But relief is imperative, and among possible remedies, none of which is perfect, this appears to us to be the least problematic."[17]

4. The Critics of the National Court Proposal

The second, third and fourth recommendations of the study group have provoked little dispute. But the first recommendation, that for a new National Court, has drawn numerous critics, some of them important, some intemperate, some both, and some neither. It has drawn, it seems, nothing but critics. And no wonder. It would certainly be preferable to let things stay as they are, if one could expect they would continue to work. No one should wish to tinker with the Supreme Court out of a simple belief that everything can be improved and that nothing should remain the same forever. Change for the sake of change is altogether an abomination, particularly in the case of the judicial branch of government whose stability, more even than that of other branches, is one of the great sources of its strength.

Nor is it surprising that many people feel uneasy at the prospect of any diminution, even apparent diminution, in the function of the Supreme Court. The late Justice Robert H. Jackson once remarked that the members of the Court are infallible because they are final, not final because they are infallible. But there is a tendency nonetheless to believe that everyone else is more fallible than the justices. Yet this is only sentiment—understandable and gratifying to those

---

[17] *Report*, p. 22.

who cherish the institution, but sentiment nevertheless—not any sort of decisive consideration.

Although criticism of the study group's report has certainly predominated and has approached the dimensions of a storm, it has not been the sole reaction. There have been other voices also, not giving immediate and unqualified endorsement of the study group's principal recommendation, but soliciting open-minded consideration of it and challenging the critics at least to offer alternative solutions. Said Chief Justice Burger in an address to the American Bar Association in August 1973:

> Reasonable men can disagree over the particular kind of intermediate court recommended by [the study group] and the powers of that court, but no person who looks at the facts can rationally assume that nine Justices today can process four or five times as many cases as the Courts that included Taft, Holmes, Brandeis and Hughes—to mention only a few—and do this task as it should be done. It is a flattering thought that we of today's Court possess such extraordinary capacities, but it is a superficial reaction to a serious study. To suggest, as has been done, that additional law clerks can take up the increased load may flatter the ego of law clerks, but I suggest that the public and the profession want the decisional functions to be exercised by judges. . . . Few have challenged the existence of a grave problem, and now it is the plain duty of the profession to explore all possible avenues for solutions. Sterile, negative criticism is of little use to anyone, and it is the obligation of those who disagree with the solutions proposed to offer their own alternatives. I will continue to defer my conclusions on this subject until I see the alternatives.

Speaking to the Fourth Circuit Judicial Conference in June 1972, before the study group report was issued, Mr. Justice Powell warned that "the steadily increasing caseload [of the Supreme Court]—a trend which shows no sign of abatement . . . may soon reach the point when the competency and craftsmanship of the Court will be perceptibly affected." In April 1973, in a talk to the Fifth Circuit Judicial Conference a few months after the report had been published, Justice Powell said that the "indispensable condition for the discharge of the Court's responsibility," as defined by the study group, "simply does not exist." The report, Justice Powell went on, had addressed the present problems of the Court "as an institution [that] we all revere." These problems "now merit the best thinking of our profession."

"It seems rather obvious to me," Mr. Justice Rehnquist has remarked, "that the adoption of the [study group's] proposal would save the Supreme Court some of the time it now spends in screening cases and that the time so saved could be devoted to deliberation and writing opinions in cases heard and decided." He added that he meant to express no judgment "as to whether the remedy proposed [by the study group] is the most desirable one available. But whatever may be the ultimate national judgment about the proposed solution, we surely must not shrink from facing the problem it outlines merely because an effective solution would require a change in the method by which the Supreme Court does business."[18]

The Advisory Council for Appellate Justice, a group of state and federal judges and lawyers and scholars engaged in a long-range study of appellate procedure, concluded at a meeting in New Orleans in February 1973: "The A.C.A.J. is persuaded that the Supreme Court's mounting case load poses a problem of growing seriousness. The [study group's] thoughtful assessment of the problem and its conclusion that some remedial measures are necessary are convincing."

Still, the critical voices have certainly been more numerous. The main grounds of objection have been the following:

(1) Contrary to the study group's conclusion, no need for relief has been shown, certainly no imperative need. "The case for our 'overwork' is a myth," Mr. Justice Douglas went out of his way to remark in a dissent issued just as the study group's report was coming out. The increase in the caseload, he continued, had been largely in the category of in forma pauperis cases, filed by prisoners free of cost and often without benefit of counsel. Most such cases are wholly frivolous and extraordinarily few of them are ever accepted for review. They burden no one. "We are," said the justice, "if anything, underworked, not overworked." The Court disposes of "vast leisure time."[19]

Former Chief Justice Warren declared that the study group's "facile and unevaluated use of numbers, reminiscent of the McCarthy days, leaves the public with a false impression as to the workload of the Court and the ability of the justices to manage that workload." He also emphasized the large number of in forma pauperis cases and added that more than half of the rest of the docket consisted of cases that "were equally without *certiorari* merit and were doubtless denied with a minimum expenditure of the justices' time and effort."[20] Mr.

---

[18] W. H. Rehnquist, "The Supreme Court: Past and Present," *American Bar Association Journal*, vol. 59 (April 1973), pp. 361, 363-364.

[19] Tidewater Oil Co. v. United States, 409 U.S. 151, 174, 176, 177 (1972).

[20] Warren and Burger, "Warren Attacks, Burger Defends," pp. 724, 726.

Justice Brennan stated categorically "that I spent no more time screening the 3,643 cases of the 1971 term than I did screening half as many in my first term in 1956."[21] The view that nothing at all alarming was happening to the Court's workload was shared by Eugene Gressman of the District of Columbia bar, a former law clerk and a long-time observer of the Court, and somewhat more qualifiedly by former Justice Arthur J. Goldberg.[22]

(2) Even critics who did not subscribe to Justice Douglas's view that the Court commands "vast leisure time" doubted that the justices are or need to be very heavily occupied in the task of screening cases. Hence in this view, to the extent—and it is a minimal extent—that the size of the docket as such imposes a burden, this burden can be lightened by remedies much less radical than the study group's proposal. The study group itself, in its other three recommendations, suggested remedies that might well be sufficient. Judge Friendly added that the justices might find it possible to dispose of petitions for certiorari more speedily, on the basis of one-sentence memoranda from their law clerks or just a few minutes' talk with them. Or else, he wrote, the justices could pool their clerks, which as noted earlier a few of them are doing on an experimental basis, instead of each getting a memorandum on each case from one of his own clerks. Then again, the justices could have more clerks or a small senior staff. Any of these suggestions, Judge Friendly maintained, "or a combination of them, would save an enormous amount of time of the justices and their clerks, yet would keep control of the Court's docket where it ought to be." But Judge Friendly's conclusion, although uncompromisingly adverse to the study group's recommendation, was more cautious than his arguments: "In my view, if the Court's docket can be kept at or near its present size, the proposed cure is worse than the ailment." Judge Friendly thus ended up saying less than he seemed to be: just three pages earlier, if not quite in the same breath, he had expressed the opinion that before the end of the decade some 3,400 petitions for certiorari—"as many as the Court's entire filings for the 1969 Term"—would reach the Supreme Court from the federal courts of appeals alone.[23]

---

[21] W. J. Brennan, "Justice Brennan Calls National Court of Appeals Proposal 'Fundamentally Unnecessary and Ill Advised,'" *American Bar Association Journal*, vol. 59 (August 1973), pp. 835, 837.

[22] See E. Gressman, "The National Court of Appeals: A Dissent," *American Bar Association Journal*, vol. 59 (March 1973), pp. 253, 254; A. J. Goldberg, "One Supreme Court," *New Republic*, February 10, 1973, pp. 14, 15; see also N. Lewin, "Helping the Court with Its Work," *New Republic*, March 3, 1973, pp. 15, 16.

[23] Friendly, *Federal Jurisdiction*, pp. 50-51, 48; see above, footnote 5.

Mr. Eugene Gressman also suggested that the addition of more clerks or the creation of a senior professional staff might constitute adequate solutions, and he commented that limiting the length of petitions for review and briefs in opposition to them to "say five to ten pages," instead of the present common length of perhaps twenty or twenty-five, might go a substantial way towards solving whatever problem exists. Finally he suggested that the Court might sit in panels of three for consideration of petitions, each panel making a report and recommendation to the entire Court.[24] Mr. Nathan Lewin, sometime law clerk to the late Justice Harlan and a former assistant to the solicitor general, has proposed that the Court might conserve time and energy by deciding many more cases than it now does in summary fashion, without hearing argument and without writing opinions.[25]

(3) A common theme among the critics is that the study group's proposal would entail a loss of control, as Chief Justice Warren put it, over "national priorities in constitutional and legal matters."[26] The study group itself noted its awareness that "some measure of loss of control by the Supreme Court" would necessarily be involved, commenting that this was "inevitable if the Court's burden is to be lessened" and that the proposal, in the study group's opinion, involved "the least possible loss of control."[27]

In the critics' view, more than just "a measure" of control would be lost, and the consequences would be grave. The flow of petitions for review, it has been argued, enables the Court to keep its finger on the pulse of the legal order. "Across the screen each Term," wrote Mr. Justice Douglas, "come the worries and concerns of the American people—high and low—presented in concrete, tangible form."[28] Chief Justice Warren observed: "The very flow of those cases through the chambers of the Court serves to inform the justices of what is happening to the system of justice."[29]

Occasional dissents by one or more justices from a denial of review, Justice Brennan pointed out, "often herald the appearance on the horizon of a possible reexamination" of previously settled law. The judges of the new National Court would have and could acquire no sense of such impending changes. Only the justices of the Supreme

---

[24] Gressman, "National Court of Appeals," p. 255.

[25] Lewin, "Helping the Court," p. 19.

[26] Warren and Burger, "Warren Attacks, Burger Defends," p. 728.

[27] Report, p. 23.

[28] Tidewater Oil Co. v. United States, 409 U.S. 151, 175.

[29] Warren and Burger, "Warren Attacks, Burger Defends," p. 729.

Court in their own assessment of their own collective thinking can know what changes may be trembling on the brink. If the flow of petitions for review should be diverted from the justices and the justices deprived of the opportunity to signal what is in their minds through an occasional dissent, then currents of change in the law will be dammed before they are fairly started, and the intellectual leadership that the Court must give the profession will be impaired.[30]

When the justices are ready to initiate a change in the law, moreover, they may be deprived of the opportunity to do so—not merely to discuss or signal a possible change, but actually to make it— because the cases which would serve as the vehicles of change will not be available to them, having been stopped in the new National Court before they could come to the notice of the Supreme Court. The judges of the new court, wrote Chief Justice Warren, being necessarily "trained to follow precedent," would "deny review of those decisions that fall into the traditional molds and that seem correctly decided in terms of precedent and settled law."[31] Former Justice Goldberg thought it doubtful that many of the cases in which the Court in the 1960s reformed various aspects of criminal procedure, or the recent death penalty case, or even the first legislative apportionment case (Baker v. Carr), or indeed Brown v. Board of Education would ever have reached the Supreme Court from a new National Court of Appeals. Moreover, Chief Justice Warren added, there are cases which should not be granted review but in which summary justice needs to be done. "There are many instances where the Court, without granting plenary review, has summarily reversed, remanded, or taken other direct action to achieve what the justices conceived to be essential justice. Much of this power would disappear under the study group's proposal. Both the Court and those who are oppressed or who are victims of miscarriages of justice would be the poorer."[32] In sum, wrote Justice Douglas, "processing"—as he called it—the mass of cases that comes before the Court is important work, "and in many ways it is the most important work we do. For the selection of cases across the broad spectrum of issues presented is the very heart of the judicial process."[33]

(4) The other side of the coin of loss of control by the Court is loss of access to it, and the objection to the proposal on the ground

---

[30] Brennan, "National Court of Appeals Proposal," p. 838.

[31] Warren and Burger, "Warren Attacks, Burger Defends," p. 729.

[32] Ibid.

[33] Tidewater Oil Co. v. United States, 409 U.S. 151, 175.

of loss of access has been perhaps most fully stated by former Justice Goldberg:

> There is the greatest value in citizens being able to believe that, as a matter of principle, every man and woman has a right to take a claim involving basic rights and liberties to the Supreme Court of the United States. It is this belief that in part inspires the great popular reverence for the Supreme Court in its role as "a palladium of liberty," and a "citadel of justice." Even though, as a practical matter, most claims will not strike the Justices as significant enough to warrant plenary consideration, it is important to the sustenance of this view that litigants know that the Justices have at least looked at, and evaluated, their claim, and that every citizen knows that he has the right to have the Justices themselves pass upon his claim.[34]

Chief Justice Warren, making the same point, said the Court "would lose its symbolic but vitally important status as the ultimate tribunal to which all citizens, poor or rich, may submit their claims." [35]

(5) Closely connected to the argument just mentioned is a question of constitutionality raised by Chief Justice Warren, Justice Goldberg and Mr. Gressman. The study group's proposal, they have said, without relieving the Supreme Court of any jurisdiction, as Congress is perhaps authorized to do, would cause the jurisdiction of the Court to be shared in certain cases with the new National Court of Appeals. Yet Article III of the Constitution provides for "one supreme Court." Having vested jurisdiction in the single allowable Supreme Court, Congress could not, Justice Goldberg wrote, "delegate to another court the responsibility of determining which cases the Supreme Court will hear." [36] The power to decide cases, which would remain in the Supreme Court, presupposes the power to determine what cases will be decided. So also Mr. Gressman: the proposal, he wrote, is not to remove any of the Supreme Court's jurisdiction but to transfer to a lower court the exercise of part of it. "There's the constitutional rub." [37] And Chief Justice Warren asked: "When the jurisdiction of the Supreme Court is exercised by two courts, have we not created two Supreme Courts" in contravention of the constitutional provision for one Supreme Court? [38]

---

34 Goldberg, "One Supreme Court," p. 16.
35 Warren and Burger, "Warren Attacks, Burger Defends," p. 727.
36 Goldberg, "One Supreme Court," p. 16.
37 Gressman, "National Court of Appeals," p. 255.
38 Warren and Burger, "Warren Attacks, Burger Defends," p. 729.

(6) On another tack, criticism was addressed to the nature and composition of the proposed new National Court and to the effect of its establishment on the existing courts of appeals. The National Court, composed by a random method—a kind of "gadgetry," not designed to recruit the best-qualified judges but only to reflect an average—would not be likely to inspire confidence, least of all in the existing courts of appeals and in the state courts, wrote Judge Friendly. "One does not like to imagine what Judge Learned Hand would have said about having his decisions reviewed by anything like the National Court." [39] The new court, Chief Justice Warren wrote, "could have no meaningful cohesion, continuity, or *esprit de corps*. . . . Most of the time, the new court would not be acting as a court; it . . . would be acting essentially as a National Court of Glorified Law Clerks. There would be little challenge or interest or enthusiasm. . . . " [40] The same point has been made by others, notably in a bar association address by Professor Paul Bator of Harvard Law School, and privately by a number of judges of the present courts of appeals.

5. A Rebuttal

As of now, more than seventy cases arrive in the Supreme Court every week of the year, including the weeks of the Court's summer recess. That is how the figure on cases filed annually breaks down when divided by fifty-two, and that, give or take a few cases, is how it actually works out in practice. Each case, whether on appeal or certiorari, consists of a brief asking the Court to grant review and most often, certainly in cases not filed by indigents, of a reply brief opposing review. Commonly a brief will run to some twenty pages. Mr. Gressman, we saw, suggests that briefs might be cut down to five or ten. But a case must be allowed to explain itself and its legal environs if any sort of intelligent disposition is to be made of it, and five to ten pages will not always suffice, especially since one or two pages at least are taken up with formal but nonetheless essential recitals. The Court used to require the filing as well of an appendix giving relevant portions of the record in the case, but that requirement was dropped a few years ago, obviously in an effort to reduce the volume of paper.

---

[39] Friendly, *Federal Jurisdiction*, pp. 52-53.

[40] Warren and Burger, "Warren Attacks, Burger Defends," p. 729.

Of course the cases vary in importance and complexity. The nub of many of them is quickly grasped, and the justices unquestionably develop a "feel" for what is worthy of consideration and what is not. Many cases, no doubt a majority, are plainly unsuitable for Supreme Court review. Looked at from the point of view of their eligibility for ultimate decision in the Supreme Court of the United States—and the sole duty of the justices with respect to these cases is to look at them from that point of view—a great many are trivial, many even frivolous. And that is especially true of in forma pauperis cases, filed by indigents, mostly prisoners. But the growth of the Court's docket is by no means accounted for by in forma pauperis cases alone, nor does a reasonably projected line of further growth point in the in forma pauperis direction.

The increase in filings of in forma pauperis cases has been dramatic, to be sure. Since 1958, these cases have accounted for more than half the total number of cases filed for review. This is not to say, however, that the increase in nonindigent cases has failed to keep pace. The number of paid, nonindigent cases filed at the October term, 1972, was substantially greater than the total number of cases, paid and unpaid, filed fifteen years earlier. Moreover, the explosion in the filings of in forma pauperis cases occurred during the 1960s. Since then, their growth rate has tapered off and is now roughly even with that of nonindigent cases. At the 1969, 1970 and 1971 terms, nonindigent cases showed a greater increase and, although the increase was again greater in the indigent category at the 1972 term, the difference was only some thirty cases.

For the purposes for which the Supreme Court is required to deal with them, then, many of the cases are easily dealt with, especially since many are in forma pauperis cases. But somebody's fate does hang in the balance in each case, even though the case is readily seen as not being fit for review in the Supreme Court. No case can be regarded as trivial in any absolute sense. The now nearly 4,000 cases that arrive during the year are self-selected, but it takes considerable doing and considerable expense, if one can afford it, to get as far as the Supreme Court. The 4,000 cases that do get that far are a very small percentage of the total number of cases decided in the federal courts of appeals and in the highest courts of the states that could be brought up. Hence the 4,000 have to be regarded as something like the cream of the crop, and choice among them ought to be made with care.

At an average of half an hour a case, it would take more than half of a heavy working week to dispose of seventy cases arriving

each week. Undoubtedly, an average of half an hour is an over-estimate. But at fifteen minutes a case, seventy cases would take two good working days each week. Some cases may require less than fifteen minutes and some, even "an astonishing number" as former Justice Goldberg has said, may raise "questions that a third-year law student can immediately recognize as inappropriate for the Supreme Court."[41] Even so, they concern matters of importance to the parties, they were brought up at effort and expense, and they must all claim the attention of each of the nine justices, not of third-year law students. And we are talking about the average time devoted to nearly 4,000 cases—fifteen minutes, perhaps less, but not much less, per case on the average, not necessarily for each case. Some will take longer. The justices can avail themselves of assistance. "Law clerks," says Justice Goldberg, "are helpful to the Justices in summarizing and digesting" cases. But Justice Goldberg also takes care to emphasize "that every Justice does his own work and makes his own decisions, whether in passing on applications for *certiorari* or in deciding argued cases."[42]

"Lawyers," Justice Rehnquist has remarked, "are not notable for their ability either to conduct or profit from time and motion studies of their occupations, and in this regard judges are at best former lawyers."[43] But estimates, however imprecise, are possible. Chief Justice Burger, in an address to the American Law Institute in May 1973, mentioned the comment of an unnamed critic of the study group that it takes or need take no more than five or six seconds to pass on most petitions for review. Then the chief justice said:

> I am willing to assume the gentleman misspoke himself and that possibly he meant five or six minutes, but I would still reject his notion of how the Supreme Court should evaluate a petition. Some are indeed patently frivolous, but that is an evaluation calling for more than five or six seconds. We are all aware that back of a petition for certiorari may be several years of litigation in the trial courts, a large record on an appeal in which competent lawyers have spent hundreds of hours, followed in turn by a good deal of time on the petition for certiorari. I doubt that the bar of the Supreme Court—or the bar generally—would think that five or six seconds, or indeed five or six minutes, constitute the true judicial consideration contemplated by our system of justice.

---

[41] Goldberg, "One Supreme Court," p. 15.

[42] Ibid.

[43] Rehnquist, "Supreme Court: Past and Present," p. 361.

The emphasis in the chief justice's remarks is on what constitutes the true judicial consideration owed to petitions for review, and on how much time and effort the function of passing on these petitions necessarily requires if the function is to be adequately discharged. That the average time must be greater than five or six minutes per petition, let alone five or six seconds, is an objective judgment. Any informed observer who has a true conception of the nature of the function is in a position to make this judgment, and its validity would not be affected by evidence that in fact the average is often less. But in fact the best possible evidence, including the chief justice's, is that the average is more, not less.

Among justices now serving, all of whom were interviewed by the study group, not all were able, ex-lawyers that they were, to name an amount of time spent on petitions for review. A number, however, did offer estimates. Fifteen hours a week, said one senior justice. Two hours a day, in the evening, said a newer justice—who, as is common among the justices, always works evenings and a six to six-and-a-half day week. Another senior justice estimated one-fifth of his time. Yet another, up to a third. With a single exception—that of Justice Douglas, whose views are public—all of the justices reported that the workload was heavy. In no instance was the report in the nature of a complaint, and not every justice viewed the situation as having reached the dimensions of crisis. But most viewed it with concern. As Professor Freund has recalled in a speech to the American Bar Association in August 1973, one senior justice "observed that when he came to the Supreme Court from another court he thought that now he would be able, as he had not been, to plumb every case to its bottom; but, he said, that proved an illusion, since the load was even greater on the Supreme Court. But, he said, you learn to numb yourself to it." Every justice but Justice Douglas thought that the Court was working at capacity. More than one remarked that the Court was saturated, and whatever the degree of concern evoked by the present situation, there was no question that serious conditions would be confronted if the docket continued to grow.

Writing to his friend Sir Frederick Pollock in 1917, when only a relatively small part of the Supreme Court's jurisdiction was discretionary and called for examination of petitions for review, Justice Oliver Wendell Holmes explained that in each such petition

> we had to familiarize ourselves with the case so far as to decide whether it was a proper one to come up, a question, that I, at least, generally answer with very little regard to

whether the case seems to me to have been decided rightly or not. But counsel who don't know the ropes generally argue the merits at length in their briefs, and that common American long-windedness presents us with volumes like the Bible. I don't read more than is necessary, but on top of the work in court it is a job.[44]

Four years later, still before the conversion of the major part of the Court's jurisdiction to a discretionary one, Holmes remarked upon his return to Washington after the summer recess that he had "begun upon the great number of applications for *certiorari* (in cases that depend on our discretion for the right to come up) that always await us—a big job. . . ."[45] And in 1929, four years after the Judges' Bill had become law, he explained again to Pollock:

> We have to consider the *certiorari* because it was only after effort that we got a bill passed that makes an appeal to our court dependent upon our discretion in many cases in which until lately it was a matter of right. Let it ever be understood that the preliminary judgment was delegated, I should expect the law to be changed back again very quickly with the result that we would have to hear many cases that have no right to our time; as it is we barely keep up with the work.[46]

What can have changed since Holmes's day to make it possible or acceptable for the justices now to spend a tiny, hardly measurable fraction of their time and effort on petitions for review and to deal with them, as former Chief Justice Warren would have it, "almost instinctively,"[47] or as Mr. Gressman tells us, to "quickly learn to take short cuts in their consideration of the many petitions," finding the disposition of the vast majority of them "immediately obvious"? Mr. Gressman says that the justices "find it unnecessary to read every word of a 50-page petition," but so did Justice Holmes, and yet the relatively very small number of petitions he confronted struck him as "a big job."[48]

We have the word of Mr. Nathan Lewin for the proposition that disposing of some seventy petitions for review per week is no great

---

[44] Mark D. Howe, ed., *Holmes-Pollock Letters*, vol. 1 (Cambridge: Harvard University Press, 1946), p. 247.

[45] Ibid., vol. 2, p. 79.

[46] Ibid., p. 251.

[47] Warren and Burger, "Warren Attacks, Burger Defends," p. 727.

[48] Gressman, "National Court of Appeals," p. 225.

trick. The late Justice Felix Frankfurter, says Mr. Lewin, used to "scan the petitions quickly himself. . . . In fact it was reported in the Court that the Justice would take the full load of petitions home one night a week and leaf through them while lying in bed."[49] The present writer was law clerk to Mr. Justice Frankfurter at the October term, 1952. He can testify that the justice was busy with petitions for review, not one night a week, but many nights, and that when he had finished with them they bore his underlinings and his notations. The justice was always surrounded by them. Stacks of them were forever piled in his study, and mailsacks full of them were shipped in and out of the small summer home he and Mrs. Frankfurter rented those years in Charlemont, Massachusetts. There was no casual leafing at bedtime. And that was when the total number of cases filed was 1,283, one-third the present volume, and when the in forma pauperis cases were not generally circulated to each justice, as they now very properly are, but were screened by one of the chief justice's clerks who wrote a one-page memorandum, the original going to the chief justice and carbons, called "flimsies," to the eight associate justices. Petitions for review are often trivial or frivolous in the sense that they do not merit a hearing in the Supreme Court, but comments on the Court's workload and method of operation ought not to be.

Mr. Justice Stewart is reported in a law school student newspaper to have remarked that the present Supreme Court workload is "neither intolerable nor impossible to handle."[50] "Intolerable," "impossible"—these are words chosen with care, and they do no more than conform to the view expressed by some justices in conversations with the study group that while the Court is now at capacity or saturated, the point of acute crisis has not yet been reached. Not quite yet! In a severely adverse comment on the study group's report, Mr. Justice Brennan has said publicly that, with experience, the task of dealing with petitions for review becomes "less onerous and time-consuming" and that he spends no more time on petitions now, despite the much greater volume of them, than he did when he began his service with the Court seventeen years ago.[51] Yet Justice Brennan has also said, publicly and to the study group, that he has abandoned absolutely all outside activities of the sort that in earlier years he did engage in. Like his colleagues, he has one more law clerk than he did in

---

[49] Lewin, "Helping the Court," p. 16.

[50] *Harvard Law Record*, vol. 55, no. 8 (1972), p. 1.

[51] Brennan, "National Court of Appeals Proposal," p. 837.

1956 and he now regularly hears one hour of argument in cases taken by the Court for decision, as compared with the two hours that the Court allowed in 1956. But the Court hears and decides no more cases now than then. The extra assistance and the extra time must have been needed for something. Moreover, as Professor Freund remarked to the American Bar Association in August 1973, given Justice Brennan's statement that he spends as much time now on nearly 4,000 petitions for review as he spent when newly appointed on less than half that number, "it is difficult to see how he could function if he were newly appointed today."

Only Mr. Justice Douglas of the justices now serving has taken the position, without qualification or ambiguity, both publicly and in his interview with the study group, that the Court is neither burdened nor in any danger of becoming so, that it is not saturated, that it does not operate at capacity, that it is indeed underworked. Justice Douglas has expressed this view often before, and he has acted on it. He has now been on the Court for over thirty-four years and has double the experience of the next senior justice, Justice Brennan. Moreover, Justice Douglas is endowed with a singular capacity and willingness to work rapidly. Not everyone may agree on the desirability of having a Court of nine Douglases, but there can be no dispute that we do not have such a Court and are not likely to have one in the future—nor indeed a Court composed of justices all or most of whom have seventeen years of experience. Whether the workload is tolerable is not a question to be answered by weighing the burden that falls on the most junior justice. Nor can the workload be assessed, however, from the vantage point of the most senior.

But there is another, more telling reason why the view of Justice Douglas is singular. Decision for him is quite apparently a series of high-speed, high-volume events, not the process that the study group described and sought to foster. No justice other than Justice Douglas maintains that the Court could hear argument in, and could decide, many more cases than it now hears and decides and still give each case adequate consideration, collectively and individually. But Justice Douglas does so maintain, and he maintains it extravagantly. At both its 1971 and 1972 terms, the Court heard argument in 177 cases. At both terms, Justice Douglas would have had the Court hear argument and render decision in some 460 additional cases in which he noted his dissents from denials of certiorari, dismissals of appeals, and other dispositions without argument. Nobody else dissented from the Court's refusals to set cases down for argument more than some twenty, or at most thirty, times in either of these two terms.

It is clear that if Justice Douglas is serious, as he evidently is, his conception of the nature of the Court's work diverges radically from that of all his colleagues, since there can be no other explanation of his wholly divergent estimate of the workload the Court is capable of assuming. Perhaps Justice Douglas thought that as many as half the cases in which the Court heard argument at the 1971 and 1972 terms were wrongly chosen. Still he would have the Court hear and decide at least three times more cases than it now does. His assessment of the Court's capacity departs by orders of magnitude from that of any of his colleagues. He can depart this far only because he proceeds from a different conception of the task.

In this, Justice Douglas is not entirely alone among critics of the study group's report, although he is alone in the clarity and forthrightness of his position and in his willingness to accept its full consequences. Mr. Lewin suggests that there is no such thing, nor can there be, as collegial deliberation, and that it would little matter if the justices had more time to write opinions, since it is "the bottom line" that counts. Indeed Mr. Lewin urges the Court to decide many more cases than it now does by summary reversal or affirmance, without opinion and without hearing argument. And even where briefs are submitted and the case is to be decided with opinion, what is the use in most cases, Mr. Lewin asks, of hour upon hour of oral argument? "Justice Douglas," he tells us, "spends much of that time writing opinions on other cases, but not all the justices are able to do two jobs at once (or willing to subject lawyers to that indignity)."[52] And even Judge Friendly, surprisingly enough but ambiguously, has allowed that although "the present system may waste some of the Justices' time [on petitions for review], it is scarcely possible to engage in deep constitutional contemplation all day long, and there is no specific showing that the country has suffered from this diversion of energy."[53]

To sum up the argument thus far, Justice Douglas is the author of the only full-throated assertion—free of ambiguity, ambivalence or internal contradiction and, therefore, in its own terms persuasive—that the present size and prospective growth of the Court's docket constitute no particular problem and call for no particular remedy. The issue, as drawn by Justice Douglas's position, is clear. If the task of decision is more an individual administrative or executive event than a collective scholarly and deliberative process, if in another sense of the word the Court can "process" cases after the

---

[52] Lewin, "Helping the Court," pp. 17, 19.
[53] Friendly, *Federal Jurisdiction*, p. 51.

fashion of a high-speed, high-volume enterprise, if all that counts is "the bottom line," and if a day spent in deep constitutional contemplation is a day partly wasted, then Justice Douglas is plainly right and there is no problem. Otherwise there is, or there will soon be. And no attempt to minimize the problem without accepting Justice Douglas's premise can ring true.

For those who recognize the existence of a problem, the inquiry must turn to possible remedies. Of the study group's recommendations only the one for a new National Court can meet the problem of the Court's docket, or was intended to do so, although all are important and should be acted upon. The elimination of three-judge courts and of other direct appeals and the establishment of a nonjudicial body to investigate and report on complaints of prisoners might have some marginal effect on the size of the docket and might otherwise result in some conservation of the justices' time. But the total effect would not be appreciable. Perhaps not all, but most, of the same cases would still arrive in the Supreme Court, although by a different route and in a shape that would make it easier for the justices to deal with them. The substitution of certiorari for appeal in all remaining cases where appeal is now still the prescribed procedure for review would have no effect at all on the size of the docket. Nor, of course, would improved support in the Office of the Clerk and in the library and increased secretarial help.

The various suggestions for restructuring the lower federal courts or even more far-reaching suggestions for altering their jurisdiction and thus controlling the intake of cases in the federal system must all stand or fall on their own merits. Many are eminently worthy of consideration. But again the effect on the Supreme Court's docket would, as the study group pointed out, be at best marginal, since the principal result would be merely to shift the channels through which cases reach the Supreme Court, not to foreclose access.

There remain only three types of solution. The first is the truly radical one, whose time may yet come but, in the study group's judgment, has not yet. This is the creation of a full-fledged fourth-tier appellate court and the limitation of the Supreme Court's docket to the 400 or 500 cases that the fourth-tier appellate court would decide annually. If one excludes this drastic remedy—and it has at the moment no audible advocates—the question becomes simply whether the justices as individual decision makers are to be substantially relieved of the so-called screening function by an institutionalization of that function within the Court or outside it. The study group elected to recommend the latter.

Relieving the nine individual justices and institutionalizing the screening function inside the Court could be accomplished in a number of ways. One device would be to break the Court up into panels of three, so that each justice would carry the burden of only one-third of the total docket. As the docket grew, of course, the efficacy of this solution would decrease. But the main objection to breaking the Court up into panels, the objection that was persuasive to the study group, was stated by Justice Douglas in a March 1970 address to the Association of the Bar of the City of New York. Justice Douglas's emphasis was on the division of the Court into panels for purposes of deciding cases rather than of passing on petitions for review, but his points hold no less for the latter function, especially since once the Court had begun to operate in panels for any purpose, the practice would be likely to be extended. "That procedure," said Justice Douglas, "would seemingly require, as [Chief Justice] Stone used to say, a constitutional amendment, since Article III speaks of 'one' Supreme Court. And if there were panels, the jockeying that would take place for choice of the panel to resolve a critical and controversial constitutional question would be unseemly."

Other ways of relieving the justices by institutionalizing the screening function within the Court all necessarily involve creating an explicit gap between function and responsibility. The formal responsibility would remain with the justices, but the function would be delegated effectively to an augmented staff of junior law clerks, or to senior law clerks (three justices have requested funds for senior clerks in the Court's budget for fiscal 1974), or to some other form of senior professional staff. Formally, staffs of this sort would make recommendations to the Court, or perhaps even to each individual justice, but if the scheme were to give any relief the recommendations would in effect constitute the action of the Court, subject only to the remotest kind of supervision by the justices, and to their final authority, to be sure, to discharge any member of the staff whose performance they regarded as unsatisfactory.

This would constitute, not to put too fine a point on it, bureaucratization of at least one aspect of the process of justice, and the objection to it is fundamental. "Let it ever be understood that the preliminary judgment was delegated," Holmes said four years after the enactment of the Judges' Bill, and "I should expect the law [the Judges' Bill] to be changed back again very quickly. . . ."[54] In 1959, the late Justice John Marshall Harlan expressed the same thought

---

[54] See Howe, ed., *Holmes-Pollock Letters*, vol. 2, p. 251.

when he noted that "the willingness of Congress to relinquish to the Court what in practical effect amounts to control of its appellate docket naturally presupposed that the Court would exercise this responsibility with a proper degree of deliberation. . . ."[55] Justice Louis D. Brandeis—who, when asked why the Supreme Court had always been held in such high respect would reply, "because we do our own work"—made the point passionately in a letter to his friend, the future Justice Frankfurter, just as the Judges' Bill was nearing enactment:

> Our jurisdiction bill will doubtless become a law within a few days. When it does, this story—with a moral—may well be written.
> U.S.S.C. [U.S. Supreme Court]—Venerated throughout the law. Despite the growth of population, wealth, and government functions, and development particularly of federal activities, the duties of the court have—by successive acts from time to time throughout a generation—been kept within such narrow limits that the nine men—each with one helper, can do the work as well as it can be done by men of this caliber. I.e., the official coat has been cut according to the human cloth.
> Congress, Executive Depts, commissions and lower federal courts—all subject to criticism or execration—regardless of human limitations, increasingly the work had been piled upon them at nearly every level. The high incumbents—in many cases—perform in name only. They are administrators—without time to know what they are doing or how to do it. They run human machines.[56]

Such would be the price of an internal solution to the problem of the Court's docket, the solution which is the probable alternative, the only realistic alternative, to the study group's recommendation. In the absence of any other remedy, the Court will necessarily edge in this direction. The trend may have already started, with some pooling of law clerks and possibly with the prospective employment of three senior law clerks.[57] Justice Brandeis no doubt overstated the disrepute —let alone, as he put it, the execration—that has been the fate of legislative and executive agencies where men do not do their own work. But he did not overstate the consequences that would follow upon the conversion of the Supreme Court, in whatever degree, into

---

[55] J. M. Harlan, "Some Aspects of the Judicial Process in the Supreme Court of the United States," *Australian Law Journal*, vol. 33 (1959), pp. 108, 113.

[56] Brandeis File, January–February 1925, Container 27, Felix Frankfurter Papers, Library of Congress.

[57] See footnote 15.

another administrative agency. Americans not only respect the justices because they do their own work, they also expect them to do their own work. The people understand that judging is an individual, not an institutional, function. Separation of function from responsibility by internal delegation to staff would constitute a scandal that would sap the Court's authority just as soon as people realized what had happened.

What then of the costs, which critics of the study group's recommendation deem unacceptable, of institutionalizing control of the Court's docket externally, visibly, in a body that is responsive to the Court itself but appointed independently of it and accountable publicly after the fashion of other courts? The argument that the cost is not worth paying because the relief to the justices would be minimal simply reverts to the question of whether the Court is or is not in truth overburdened. Of course no one can calculate with precision exactly how much time and energy would be conserved now, or in the future as the docket continued to grow. The evidence points to the conservation of quantities of time. Even Justice Douglas, although he believes the Court needs more business rather than less, is not in disagreement on this score. The Court's time, he says, "is largely spent in the fascinating task of reading petitions for certiorari and jurisdictional statements."[58]

Actual time—hours and days—is not the sole consideration. The proper equation is: burden $=$ time $+$ pressure. A docket of the size of the present one—seventy cases arriving each week and requiring disposition at the Friday conference—does not merely exact time; it exerts pressure which drains energy and deflects attention. Furthermore, it is not only justices' time that needs to be conserved, but also law-clerk time. The docket is converting law clerks from assistants to the justices and extensions of them in the research, discussion and deliberation required for the decision of cases into memoranda writers on petitions to review.

The theme, common to so many of the critics of the study group's report, that the benefits in time saved would be minimal is inconsistent with another equally common theme of the critics, that loss of control over its own docket would grievously impair the Court's function. It is not easy to understand how a task which takes so little time, which demands only a few seconds' attention to trivial and frivolous cases, a task that judges invited to serve on the new National Court would scorn because its performance would turn them

---

[58] Tidewater Oil Co. v. United States, p. 176.

into "Glorified Law Clerks,"[59] can also be a task so critical to the proper performance of the Court's function that to take any part of it away would be to emasculate the institution. If the flow of petitions for review to the justices' chambers informs the justices of what is happening in the system of justice, and if it is essential that they keep themselves thus informed, it cannot be that they do it by a second's glance at a petition, and it cannot be that the time and energy expended are minimal and not worth saving.

The critics cannot have it both ways. But on the assumption, which is the correct one, that exercise of control over the docket is a major task consuming time and energy, the question of what would be lost if a portion of it were given to the new National Court should be faced. No doubt the Supreme Court would lose some of the opportunities it now occasionally seizes of reversing a decision summarily, simply because the justices regard it as wrong, even though the case is otherwise of no importance to the fabric of the law and thus not deserving of Supreme Court review. Since the Court would still see somewhere in the neighborhood of 400 to 500 cases, many more than it could hear, all such opportunities would not be lost. But to the extent that they were lost, it need only be said that the function of the Court is not to correct error in individual cases, but to declare and harmonize national law. Everything else is incidental and has been conceded to be so, at least since the Judges' Bill of 1925.[60] Each case is important to the parties, and a great deal hangs for them on its acceptance or rejection by the Court. For this reason, justice requires adequate judicial consideration of each petition and of the arguments of counsel attempting to demonstrate that the case is worthy of review. But the decisive factor in that judicial consideration is the importance of the question presented to the development of national law, not whether a lower court has made an erroneous disposition of an issue that lacks general significance.

There are those, as we have seen, who fear that landmark cases, particularly those involving rights of criminal defendants, in which the Supreme Court has recently reexamined what had seemed to

---

[59] Warren and Burger, "Warren Attacks, Burger Defends," p. 729.

[60] "Under our Federal system," wrote Chief Justice Hughes in 1937, ". . . when the dissatisfied party has been accorded an appeal to the circuit court of appeals, the litigants, so far as mere private interests are concerned, have had their day in court. If further review is to be had by the Supreme Court it must be because of the public interest in the questions involved. . . . Review by the Supreme Court is thus in the interest of the law, its appropriate exposition and enforcement, not in the mere interest of the litigants." Senate Report No. 711, 75th Congress, 1st session, pp. 38-40.

be settled law would not reach the Court under the study group's recommendation because the judges of the National Court would not recognize their importance or would tend not to question established precedent. This fear is unfounded. The experienced judges of the new National Court would know that the Supreme Court sometimes reverses itself, sometimes upsets seemingly settled law, and sometimes strikes out in new directions. They would know also, as the profession knows now, that such events do not come out of the blue, altogether unexpectedly. As the study group said in its report, "the Supreme Court's readiness to reopen what had seemed to be settled issues, its impatience with, or its interest in, one or another category of cases—all this, we think, would communicate itself to the new National Court of Appeals, and would be acted upon."[61] In not one of the major cases mentioned by Justice Goldberg and other critics as unlikely to have reached the Supreme Court is it conceivable that, under the recommended system, the Court would have lacked the opportunity to make the law it actually made.

It has to be conceded, as the study group did concede, that some loss of control would be involved. The point is merely that the loss would not be critical, especially since means are provided for making the new National Court responsive to policy directions from the Supreme Court through rules that the Supreme Court could issue to govern procedures and criteria of certification in the National Court, and since the hierarchical position of the Supreme Court at the head of the federal judiciary would remain undisturbed. Means of communicating relevant attitudes of the Supreme Court exist now and would remain available, including several hundred opportunities for individual justices to file dissents from denials of review and thus signal changes in their own thinking. And the communications would be heeded. Ultimate choice of the suitable case and of the apt occasion for decision would continue to lie with the Supreme Court. There would also be a sufficient flow of cases to give the justices a sense of movements and stirrings in the legal order, which they obtain as well, of course, by keeping reasonably current with the literature of the law. No loss of control at all might be preferable. But given the problem that confronts the Court, it is not reasonable to ask whether the study group's recommendation is ideal. The reasonable question is a relative, not an absolute one, informed by the sensible attitude of the farmer who when asked how he liked his wife replied: compared to what?

---

[61] *Report*, p. 23.

To the related objection that the study group's recommendation would involve not only a loss of control on the part of the Court but a loss of access to it on the part of litigants, the answer is that very little if anything in the way of meaningful access would be lost and that, in any event, there is no a priori right of access to the Supreme Court. Senator Thomas J. Walsh of Montana, an able lawyer whose sudden death in 1933 prevented him from being Franklin D. Roosevelt's first attorney general, opposed the Judges' Bill of 1925 on the ground, among others, that it was "impossible to resist the conclusion that in the vast majority of cases [petitions for certiorari] can have nothing more than the most cursory and superficial examination."[62] That has not been the fact and has not been perceived as the fact. The consequences would have been disastrous if it had been. But it will become the fact if some such device as the one recommended by the study group is not adopted, or if control of the docket should be delegated internally to staff. If nothing is done, or if staff is resorted to, the vaunted right of access to the Supreme Court will be an illusion. It will be access, indeed, to the most cursory and superficial consideration of petitions, or else access not to judges but to an invisible staff. That is all the loss of access that adoption of the study group's recommendation would impose. Professor Freund remarked at a press conference held at the time of release of the study group report: "If the caseload increases as the Chief Justice has predicted publicly to 7,000 by 1980, what does this right [of access] consist in? It is a fine symbol and a fine ideal, but I'm afraid that so far from adding to the prestige of the Court, it will, if it gets further out of hand, become a ground of disillusionment and cynicism."

It is the birthright of Americans, say former Justice Goldberg and some other critics of the National Court proposal, to have access to the Supreme Court as a palladium of liberty and a citadel of justice. Yes, in the words with which Hemingway's *The Sun Also Rises* ends, yes, "isn't it pretty to think so?" And some people persist in thinking so, as others have before them. But it is not true. It cannot be true in a nation of over 200 million people served by one Supreme Court.

The study group recommendation would make a modest change in present procedures governing access to the Court. These procedures, though familiar for nearly half a century, were themselves, when first introduced, resisted as limiting access to the Supreme Court, as were earlier reforms also. "The establishment in 1891 of inter-

---

[62] Frankfurter and Landis, *Business of the Supreme Court*, p. 287, note 124.

mediate appellate tribunals had to overcome a deep professional feeling against taking away from litigants the right to resort to the Supreme Court for vindication of their federal claims." The assumption was widespread "that the Supreme Court was, as a matter of course, the guardian of all constitutional claims." In the end, and with difficulty, the assumption gave way to the reforms of 1891. The same "obstinate conception that the Court was to be the vindicator of all federal rights" had to be overridden by the Judges' Bill of 1925. "I find it difficult to yield to the idea," said Senator Walsh, "that the Supreme Court of the United States ought to have the right in every case to say whether their jurisdiction shall be appealed to or not." Access to the Supreme Court, he believed, at least in constitutional cases, ought to be automatic, as of right.[63] Realizing perhaps that he was merely giving voice to what Felix Frankfurter once called the tendency to "canonize the familiar into the eternal,"[64] Senator Walsh finally did yield.

The argument that creation of a National Court to screen the Supreme Court's docket would violate the provision of Article III of the Constitution for *one* supreme Court rests on a word play. The modern history of the Supreme Court, naturally enough, has been the history of the progressive curtailment of the Court's jurisdiction as the country has grown, for it has always been true, and is now, that there is only so much that a single court can do. Congress is vested by the Constitution with the authority to regulate the jurisdiction of the Supreme Court, although not for the purpose of changing substantive constitutional law. In modern times Congress has regulated that jurisdiction by excluding categories of cases in which an appeal used to lie as of right, in order to keep the docket at a manageable size. In earlier years, certain categories of cases were absolutely excluded. As we have seen, appeals were limited by the requirement of a jurisdictional amount and, until 1891, no appeal was allowed in the common run of criminal cases. In all categories of excluded cases, the decision of a lower court was final and, in making such a final decision, one could say that that lower court acted as a Supreme Court in violation of the constitutional establishment of one supreme Court.

Congress also provided, as we have seen, that certain cases come to the Supreme Court only if certified for appeal by the lower court

---

[63] Ibid., pp. 258, 260-61, 276.

[64] E. F. Prichard and A. MacLeish, eds., *Law and Politics—Occasional Papers of Felix Frankfurter* (Santa Barbara, Calif.: Capricorn Press, 1962).

which had decided them. It could have been said that in performing this function, which is precisely the function that the new National Court would perform, the certifying court was acting as another Supreme Court. But nobody said it, because quite plainly the provision for one, final, ultimate Supreme Court cannot be read to mean that all cases must be decided in it on appeal, or that it alone must decide which cases to decide, else the institution would have burst long ago. There is nothing in the Constitution to suggest that the Supreme Court itself has to determine what cases it shall decide out of an unlimited mass of possible cases. The power to decide cases, says Justice Goldberg, presupposes the power to determine what cases will be decided. This has seemed to be so because it has largely been so for the past fifty years. But it has not been so through the greater part of the history of the Republic. Judicial power to determine what cases will be decided was an innovation made by Congress for the convenience of the Court, and extended in 1925. There is nothing constitutional about it. There is something constitutional about the Court's power to refuse to decide even though Congress wishes it to, but that is an altogether different matter.

The study group recommendation for a National Court would not transfer to any other court exercise of part of the Supreme Court's jurisdiction. It would let somebody else determine, at least in part, what cases should go up to the Supreme Court for review. That is a determination that has always been made elsewhere initially, namely, by Congress, and that has been institutionalized elsewhere before now. It is not exercise of the Court's jurisdiction. Nor is there any contradiction between the study group's brushing aside the argument based on the provision for one Supreme Court so far as the establishment of the new National Court is concerned, on the one hand, and the doubt which the study group shared about the constitutionality of dividing the Supreme Court itself into panels, on the other hand. It may be that the doubt as to the latter course is overstated, although it has been widely expressed for a long time, since the suggestion of panels is not new. In any event, however, the question about panels and the question about the new National Court are separate and distinct.

It seems quite clear that many judges of the existing courts of appeals have greeted the proposal that some of them serve temporarily on the new National Court without enthusiasm. Perhaps, however, they would ultimately find service on the new court and performance of its important function, albeit arduous and inconvenient, to be a necessary public duty. No doubt, should the proposal be enacted, any judge who is asked to serve would do so with grace and with the dedication that is common to federal judges.

One troublesome criticism remains. That is the criticism that the new court would lack cohesion, continuity, and indeed identity as a court because, for the most part, it would not be engaged in the usual process of hearing argument, deliberating, and rendering decision on the merits of cases, but rather in screening. If the court is established, perhaps the importance of its function, the fact that it would have a number of cases to hear and decide on their merits each year, the growing confidence of the profession and of the country in the court's performance of its function with fidelity and skill—perhaps all that would sustain the new court as an institution. It is not visionary to hope so.

It may be added in this connection that the method proposed by the study group for organizing the new court would, as its report noted, "allow for experimentation for a period of years without a commitment to a permanent tier of judicial review and a permanent new judicial body."[65] Thus, if the hope for the court's performance and acceptance should be defeated, there would be an opportunity to improve the institution and cure its defects without having to uproot a structure designed for permanence.

Substantive law reform has striven energetically of late to enlarge rights and to secure them more widely. That also has been the aim of much recent legislation. Thus, we have increased the occasions of justice, as has the sheer growth of the country itself. But the machinery of justice, if that is what it should be called, creaks. If we should let it reach the point of breakdown or, taking the term "machinery" seriously, let it transform itself into a high-speed, high-volume enterprise, we would mock the idea of justice and mock the substantive reforms of a generation.

---

[65] *Report,* p. 24.

Cover and design: Pat Taylor